Praise for *La Grande Thérèse*

"Hilary Spurling's *La Grande Thérèse* is a work of social history in the style of Patricia Highsmith. A wonderful *petit four* after the feast of *Matisse*."

> —Elaine Showalter, author of *A Literature of Their Own: British Women Novelists from Brontë to Lessing*

"Thérèse Humbert conned her way through life, and died brazenly unrepentant. Hilary Spurling—a *grand chef* among biographers—has confected of her astounding adventures an elegant morsel of a book that will stimulate every appetite."

> —Diane Middlebrook, author of *Suits Me: The Double Life of Billy Tipton*

"There can be few characters who have managed to re-create themselves with as much daring and panache as Thérèse Daurignac. . . . The joy of this beautifully written little book is that the story reads like a novella." —*The Observer*

"Spurling is able to convey the speed and mystery of Humbert's rise and fall, giving us the sense of a fairy tale. We're left, like her victims, seduced and astounded."

> —Alice Kaplan, *New York Times Book Review*

"Her discussion of how Madame Humbert's nonexistent fortune acquired an aura of credibility rings as true in a twenty-first-century New Economy as it did in fin-de-siècle France."

> —*Kirkus Reviews*

"Hilary Spurling tells an incredible tale that, although at times high farce, is in fact all true." —*What's On in London*

"*La Grande Thérèse* is a compelling account of the life of a fanciful French peasant girl who grew up to make solid and real her girlhood castles in the air. Hilary Spurling has discovered a sensational story; this is a bravura retelling." —*House and Garden*

"Biographer Hilary Spurling is to have her long-deserved moment in the sun." —*The Independent*

"An eminently readable history made more exquisite by the mischievous relish with which Spurling tells it." —*Metro London*

"The short, sweet and fascinating true story of the scandal of a French girl who swindled herself into wealth at the turn of the century." —*Nottingham Evening Post*

"Hilary Spurling has not only found an extraordinary story but has also settled upon exactly the right way to tell it. One thing is certain: she [Thérèse] would have adored Hilary Spurling's vibrant, racy little book." —*Daily Telegraph*

" [An] intriguing study of one of France's great unsung scandals." —*Sunday Times*

"A gem." —*Globe and Mail* (Toronto)

Thérèse Humbert's best friend, Catherine Parayre, at the
Humbert weddings in Beauzelle in 1878, with her husband
and their six-year-old daughter, Amélie, who grew up to
marry the painter Henri Matisse.
(Collection of Gaetana Matisse)

La Grande Thérèse

The Greatest Scandal of the Century

Hilary Spurling

Perennial

An Imprint of HarperCollins*Publishers*

Originally published in the United Kingdom in 1999 by Profile Books Ltd. The first U.S. edition was published in 2000 by HarperCollins Publishers.

HarperCollins books may be purchased for educational, business, or sales promotional use. For information please write: Special Markets Department, HarperCollins Publishers Inc., 10 East 53rd Street, New York, NY 10022.

First Perennial edition published 2001.

Designed by Nancy B. Field

Picture research by Gráinne Kelly

The Library of Congress has catalogued the hardcover edition as follows:

Spurling, Hilary.
    La Grande Thérèse : the greatest scandal of the century / Hilary Spurling—1st ed.
      p. cm.
    ISBN 0-06-019622-X
    1. Humbert, Thérèse, b. 1856. 2. Impostors and impostature—France—Biography. 3. France—Biography. I. Title.
CT9981'2'092—dc21
[B]   99–462221

ISBN 0-06-095592-9 (pbk.)

01 02 03 04 05 ❖/RRD 10 9 8 7 6 5 4 3 2 1

Illustrations

Illustrations

Illustrations

LE JEU DU LAPIN

...DU JEU
(...OIE, IMITÉ DES GRECS)

...andis que les autres joueurs jouent 2 fois. Qui va au 31 attend ...ne rente viagère, jusqu'à ce qu'un autre vienne le délivrer de ...on espérance; il prend alors la place de cet infirme. Qui arrive ...au n° 42, s'enfuit dans le maquis de la Procédure, paie l'amende ...t retourne au n°30, il peut se fouiller. Qui arrive au 52 à la Douil-...ette, s'y goberge, jusqu'à ce que vienne le délivrer un autre filou, ...ont il prend la place. Qui échoue au 58, près de la Conciergerie, ma ...hérie, donne tout ce qu'il a dans ses poches et retourne au n° 1 re-...ommencer la petite histoire. Châtiment cruel, mais immé-...té. Pour gagner, il faut arriver au n° 63 et alors, sous peine d'amende, toute la bande des tripoteurs doit chanter, en faisant une ronde : Entrez dans la Danse. — Voyez comme on danse ! — Embrassez le lapin que vous voudrez!

Le joueur atteint par un autre change de place avec lui.

Tous les points après 63 sont marqués à reculons.

Thérèse Daurignac was born in 1856 in the far southwest of France, in the province called Languedoc, once celebrated for its troubadours and their romances. Life for Thérèse in the little village of Aussonne, just outside Toulouse, was anything but romantic. She was the eldest child in a poor family: a stocky, bright-eyed little girl, not particularly good-looking, with nothing special about her except the power of her imagination. Thérèse told stories. In an age without television, in a countryside where most people still could not read, she transformed the narrow, drab, familiar world of the village children into something rich and strange. From their earliest years she entertained her five siblings with tales in which their father became the Comte d'Aurignac, Thérèse herself stood to inherit a fortune, and the family's modest farmhouse turned into a château.

Every house Thérèse ever inhabited became a château in her mind's eye. The first of her pure inventions was the Château de Marcotte, which stood on gleaming marble pavements among flower gardens and walks lined with orange trees on shady slopes above the sea where the Pyrenees mark the border between France and Spain. It was as far as a child's imagination could reach from the hot, dusty inland plain around Aussonne. A trip to the mountains fifty miles to the west, or to the Mediterranean coast nearly a hundred miles to the south, would have taken many days by cart or horseback along the stony tracks of Languedoc. For peasant children growing up in the flat, featureless fields behind Toulouse, Marcotte and its castle by the sea might as well have been in fairyland.

When Thérèse was small, she invented palaces for her siblings to live in, and once she was grown up, her castles in the air came true. In her prime she moved her whole family into a stately mansion with

Landscape, Toulouse, 1899, pen-and-ink drawing by Henri
Matisse, who married the daughter of Thérèse's best friend
and spent part of his honeymoon sketching and painting
the flat fields around Aussonne. *(Private collection;*
© H. Matisse/DACS London, 1999; photo: Archives Matisse,
Paris; all rights reserved)

marble halls full of fine paintings and gilt furniture
in the wealthiest part of Paris. They spent summers
in one or another of her country houses, each surrounded by its own parkland and hunting grounds

or vineyards. La Grande Thérèse, as she was called, remained for twenty years one of the most conspicuous and powerful women in France. Parisian high society vied for her favors. It was a fairy-tale outcome for an uneducated village girl born at the bottom of the social heap, with her imagination as her only capital.

Thérèse's parents were bastards. Her father had been a foundling, discovered as a baby in a church tower in Toulouse and promptly turned over to the local orphanage. Nameless babies born out of wedlock in the back streets or outlying villages of a city like Toulouse had no civil rights, no papers, and no prospects. The boy, Guillaume Auguste, belonged to nobody, and made up for it by hanging around the church, which was the only home he knew. He was finally taken in by the parish priest (generally supposed to be his natural father), who taught him to serve mass, made the most of his strong singing voice, and encouraged his taste for dressing up by putting him in charge of church vestments. Auguste went on to become for fifteen years a bishop's valet.

He acquired an identity of his own for the

first time at the age of thirty-eight, when a respectable Toulouse matron, the widow Doyen, officially claimed him as her son, giving him her maiden name, Daurignac. She had been comfortably provided for by her late husband, who was a clock- and watchmaker, but the new Auguste Daurignac welcomed this long-lost mother without enthusiasm. He had provided himself with a rather more romantic ancestry in the private dreamworld into which he could retreat as if by magic. The local people recognized him as a visionary, someone out of the ordinary, part simpleton, part sorcerer, to be treated warily for fear he would make mischief or cast spells. He was a courtly figure, frock-coated, top-hatted, at once formal and flamboyant: something of a catch when, in 1852 at the age of fifty-one, he finally married Lucie Rosa Capella, who was half his age.

Rosa was herself the illegitimate daughter of a rich farmer called Duluc. A wily operator with a reputation as both a libertine and a skinflint, old Father Duluc was famous for having gotten the better of a highwayman who held him up on the way home from market. Far from making off with the farmer's bags of gold, the would-be mugger was forced to accept a check instead, only to find the police waiting for him when he called at the bank to cash it. Rosa's mother was Madame Capella, the wife of another valet. Duluc, who never married, fathered many offspring, all of whom grew up hoping to come into his substantial fortune. In the end he left everything to his favorite of Madame Capella's three daughters, a young Madame Dupuy, who celebrated her good luck by presenting each of her sisters with a dowry of one thousand francs.

Rosa Daurignac invested her money in a farmhouse called L'Oeillet at Aussonne, where her husband proposed to earn a living as a freelance bone setter, marriage broker, and faith healer. The country people of Languedoc still lived by the seasonal rhythms, rituals, and superstitions of the Middle Ages, virtually untouched as yet by the new world of industrial expansion already beginning to transform ancient cities like Toulouse.

The Daurignacs stood out in the village. Not exactly landowners, they did not fit easily into the community of laborers, smallholders, and tenant farmers who scraped a meager living from the soil. A girl and two boys were born in quick succession: Thérèse, Emile, and Romain Daurignac. Their father solved the family's social problem by taking on a new role—a part he felt himself born to play—as unofficial lord of the manor.

But the peasants who were his clients paid little or nothing. Debts mounted, and the Daurignacs' income remained at best sporadic. Rosa, who was not her father's daughter for nothing, took out a mortgage on her house, moved into town with her little daughter, and opened a boutique selling high-class lingerie to the wives of wealthy industrialists on one of the smartest shopping streets in Toulouse. The business grew in the 1860s, and so did the family. Another boy, Louis, was followed by two more girls: Marie-Louise and Maria. The Daurignacs might have prospered if their mother had not died prematurely at L'Oeillet in January 1871, leaving her small children and their elderly father with no money coming in and no one to look after them but the fourteen-year-old Thérèse.

Over the next few years the family's situation

Thérèse's childhood dreams come true: Thérèse, pictured at the height of her fame as a society hostess in Paris, with her husband, Frédéric Humbert; her only daughter, Eve; and her younger sister, Maria Daurignac. *(Photo: © Topham Picturepoint)*

went from bad to worse. Auguste Daurignac withdrew into himself, sunk in fantasy, ignoring creditors or fending them off with talk of unspecified legal documents in a locked chest and, failing that, with the threat of magic powers. He pored over a seventeenth-century recipe book, said to be a work of alchemy containing instructions for wreaking havoc on his neighbors or, alternatively, granting their hearts' desire. He told fortunes, prophesied good or bad harvests, hinted at possession of a mighty secret. The villagers, who had accepted Daurignac's eccentricities as relatively harmless in his wife's lifetime, now looked on him uneasily as a necromancer. People remembered him in his seventies running across the fields, wild-eyed and waving a wand, in thunderstorms he claimed to have conjured up himself. Many assumed he was the children's grandfather. "He was a great booby, a good-for-nothing, he had *no* control over his children," said a barber called Bérard, who first came across the Daurignacs just before their mother's death, when things began to go wrong for them. "The head of the family was Thérèse."

Old Father Daurignac could still extract an occasional offering—a pat of butter, a basket of eggs, perhaps a chicken or a brace of game—from poor farmers who half believed in his ability to blight their crops by calling down rain or hailstones. But it was left to Thérèse to beg, borrow, and scrounge the family's daily living. Emile and

Romain followed her lead. "She was a bright little thing in those days," said Bérard: "very talkative, already—after her mother died—running the whole outfit." Thérèse fed the children, mothered the baby, and kept everybody's spirits up with her tall stories. Friends and neighbors were touched by her buoyancy and courage. Bérard was one of her earliest admirers. Another was the curé, Abbé Piette, whose support counted for much in Aussonne. A third was the bailiff's daughter, Catherine Fuzié, a dark-eyed beauty with the air of hauteur and reserve that traditionally conceals deep feeling among the women of her native South.

Catherine's fierce protective instincts responded unconditionally to Thérèse, who was eight years younger. The two had known one another as long as either could remember. "I practically brought her up," the older girl said long afterward. Catherine had been bowled over from the beginning by this marvelous, rash, reckless child, who somehow managed to give a golden glow to the lives of everyone around her. It was not simply that Thérèse's stories offered a romantic future in which they would all end up rich. Her dreams of splendor were not at this stage primarily materialistic. She opened up possibilities that were ampler, freer, and incomparably more exciting than the dull daily grind available in Aussonne. It was a liberating vision, and Catherine committed herself to it with the passionate intensity of a nature that needed to serve some purpose larger than her own immediate concerns. Before the two ever left their village, they had laid the foundations of a pact that would carry them triumphantly through twenty years of struggle to heights even Thérèse could hardly have envisaged at the start, before disaster finally engulfed them both.

✥⟡✥

Thérèse's tricks and treats added drama, zest, and conspiratorial excitement to her girlfriends' lives. They hatched plots, staged scenes, and mounted charades under her direction. At one point Thérèse persuaded the other girls to pool their bits of jewelry because, as she said with an ingenuous lisp: "People will think I've got bags of jewels, if I change them often enough."

Catherine Fuzié, the bailiff's beautiful daughter,
who believed in Thérèse from the beginning.

Another time, when guests arrived to hear her play the piano, she explained that she was too shy to perform in public, retiring to the next room where a musical friend played the piece for her, whereupon Thérèse modestly reappeared to take her bow. Performances like this one sprang from the sheer love of make-believe and mystification for their own sakes. But they were also practical rehearsals for the far more elaborate conjuring feats Thérèse would pull off in later life. "She was still so young in those days," said an observer, "that people just laughed at her showing off, and her childish lies."

Thérèse was following in the footsteps of her father, who had returned to his old dreams of a noble ancestry and a lost heritage, claiming to have proofs of both in the chest full of yellowing parchment that, according to Thérèse, dominated her childhood. A locked coffer containing crucial documents would be a constant element in the games Thérèse played out ever afterward, along lines laid down early by her father. In her teens and early twenties she talked often about a legacy from a mysterious well-wisher. Sometimes the donor was a retired village schoolmistress, living a day's drive

GRANDEUR ET DÉCADENCE DE MADAME HUMBERT (1)

Thérèse in her prime, portrayed in the popular press
as a conjurer pulling rabbits out of a hat in front of the
famous Humbert strongbox, said to contain a fortune.
(Photo: © Collection Viollet, Paris)

away in Rabastens, or a godmother from Le Havre. Once it was a rich Dutch aunt. Perhaps Thérèse's imaginary bequest had something to do with her mother's failure to inherit Farmer Duluc's money; and perhaps her string of phantom benefactors played variations on her real aunt, her mother's wealthy sister Madame Dupuy, who in fact made no move to help her hard-up nieces and nephews. Madame Dupuy came in handy instead as a figment of Thérèse's consoling fictions. The barber Bérard, whose father had been one of Duluc's many creditors, said that, even as a small girl, Thérèse could always wheedle a loan out of him by promising to get her Aunt Dupuy to honor her grandfather's outstanding debts.

All her life Thérèse treated money as an illusion: a confidence or conjuring trick that had to be mastered. In the years of poverty that followed her mother's death, she never let lack of funds stand in her way. Wild rumors about her father now began to be outdone by wilder ones about his daughter. "I'd always heard talk of the Daurignacs," said Bérard, who followed the family's fortunes avidly, regularly tuning in with the rest of the neighbors

AFFAIRE HUMBERT-CRAWFORT

DEFENSE
D'OUVRIR !!!

1. — Ils sont là !!!...

Another popular cartoon showing Thérèse with her locked
strongbox and one of her dream castles in the background.
(Photo: © Collection Viollet, Paris)

to catch the latest episode in a soap opera that
seemed altogether too well plotted for real life.
Thérèse galvanized the whole countryside with
her escapades, excursions, and flirtations. Never
exactly pretty, she prided herself when young on a
neat waist, slender ankles, and a trim figure. She

looked her best in a close-fitting riding habit that mesmerized the young farmers for miles around. She planned picnics and riding parties, gave dinners and musical evenings, borrowed a coach for pleasure trips that nobody ever forgot.

Her reputation spread first to nearby villages like Beauzelle and Blagnac, then to Toulouse itself. People had never known anything like it. Thérèse's wide-eyed innocence was especially disarming. She gave the impression of being constantly surprised by everything. Even the most suspicious were captivated by her trustfulness and evident lack of guile. She had the hesitant, husky, seductive voice of the true *Toulousaine,* and her lisp made her irresistible. "As we say in these parts," wrote another compatriot: "You would have given her the Good Lord without hearing her confession."

Certainly the dressmakers, bootmakers, hatters, and hairdressers of Toulouse were no match for the young Thérèse. "I'll pay you [*Ze vous paierai*]," she said with her ingenuous air and her adorable lisp: "I'll pay you as soon as I get my inheritance." When her debts mounted to such dizzy heights that the tradespeople's resistance stiffened, she staged her most ambitious coup to date: Thérèse was seventeen when she announced her engagement to the son of a Bordeaux shipping magnate, explaining in floods of tears that it was a loveless match she must force herself to go through with in order to honor a pact made in her infancy between their two fathers. She wept so piteously that it was only after an elaborate trousseau had been ordered, made to measure, and delivered to Aussonne, that the Toulouse shopkeepers slowly realized they had been diddled once again. Since there was no fiancé, there would be no wedding, and no well-heeled father-in-law to pick up the tabs.

It was this affair that tipped the scale. Tradesmen, who had put up with being tricked and exploited for years, rose up together in revolt. Streams of creditors, duns, and bailiffs converged on L'Oeillet. Bankruptcy could no longer be staved off. By 1874 the family was in the hands of the receiver, their house sold and its contents repossessed. The Daurignacs left Aussonne in disgrace to look for work in Toulouse. The two elder boys found low-grade jobs, Emile as a piano salesman,

The city of Toulouse, where Thérèse practiced and perfected the magical art of true romance.

Romain as a shop assistant. Ten-year-old Louis was packed off to a school run by Trappist monks. Places were arranged for the two little girls at an academy, where their bills were seldom paid at the end of the school term.

Thérèse, powerless to prevent the family's ruin and dispersal, was now publicly dependent on the uncertain charity of creditors. Each morning she stopped off with her empty shopping basket to touch Monsieur Bérard for a few coins with which to see herself and her father through the day. "I couldn't let them starve," he said, "so I always gave her something. Even reduced to penury, she still kept the airs of a young lady." She rented wretched rooms with a few sticks of broken furniture high up under the roof of a cheap lodging house in the rue de Taur. Thérèse's motto in later life was a flat statement: "What I want, I will have [*Je veux, j'aurai*]." To some it smacked of ruthless greed. But to people who had known her in these years of humiliation and defeat—when she had failed to keep a roof over the children's heads and could no longer even be sure where their next meal was coming from—it seemed more like whistling in the dark.

❧❧

None of her Toulouse relatives wanted anything to do with a family that had brought fresh shame to the already notorious name of Daurignac.

Besides Madame Dupuy, Thérèse had a second aunt, another of Farmer Duluc's penniless bastards, who had started out in the 1850s by earning her living as a maid. Marie-Emilie Thénier (or Tenière) had worked at 3, rue de Pomme, in the same house as her half-sister, Thérèse's mother, Rosa Daurignac, who sold lingerie on the ground floor. Both sisters were forceful, brave, and energetic, but it was the maid of all work who pulled off what turned out to be by far the more advantageous match. Marie-Emilie married the young law teacher whose lodgings she looked after above the shop in the rue de Pomme. Her husband was Gustave Humbert, a highflier with political ambitions who became Professor of Roman Law at the University of Toulouse, going on ten years later to be elected to the House of Representatives in Paris as the local deputy for Haute-Garonne.

The Humberts had two children, Frédéric and Alice, who were roughly the same age as their cousins Thérèse and Emile Daurignac. The four children grew up together. Thérèse by her own account was the childhood sweetheart of her cousin Frédéric, who wooed her with a ring made of polished tin. Even after Deputy Humbert moved to Paris to further his political career, he brought his family back every summer to the country outside Toulouse. They had a house beside the church at Beauzelle, where Frédéric's father quickly singled out the clever young schoolmaster, Armand Parayre, whose wife, Catherine, had been Thérèse's great friend in Aussonne. Parayre became Humbert's confidential secretary and Latin tutor to young Frédéric.

❧❧❧

The Humberts' fortunes rose in the early 1870s as the Daurignacs' went downhill. Deputy Humbert was one of the constitutional pioneers who laid the foundation stones for the Third Republic, after France's catastrophic defeat by Germany at the start of the decade. The new republic represented a fresh start for the whole country: a modern, secular, democratic state liberated at last from the stranglehold of the Roman Catholic Church as well as from the imperial folly that had ended with the downfall of Napoleon III.

Thérèse's uncle, Senator Gustave Humbert,
who rose to be the Third Republic's most
celebrated minister of justice.

Deputy Humbert was made a senator, or life mem-
ber of the newly established upper house, in 1875.

Young Frédéric was seventeen years old that
year, studying law in his first term at Toulouse
University, where his fellow students remembered
him as a dull, bookish lad with artistic leanings. He
founded a literary review for which his cousin

Emile Daurignac wrote articles. Frédéric was not stupid, but he was timid: in every way a paler, feebler, flatter version of his father. It was Thérèse who shone. Thérèse had a will to match her uncle's, and the enterprise to make the most of it. All their lives she would be the fixed post for Frédéric's clinging vine. Thérèse was eighteen, and destitute in 1875. She had also lost her power base. For the first time she found herself discredited imaginatively as well as financially in the eyes of everyone she knew. Drastic action was called for.

Four years after the Daurignac disaster, Thérèse and her brother Emile married the two young Humberts in a double wedding at Beauzelle.

The wedding celebrations on September 7, 1878, were by far the grandest spectacle the village had ever seen. People still talked about them well into the next century. The houses were decked with flowers, triumphal arches spanned the street, and the whole countryside turned out to watch the carriage procession. These were the first carriages to reach Beauzelle (which was not much more than a collection of market gardens beside the Garonne River), and the horses had to be unharnessed so that the bridal coach could be hauled by hand up the steep slope to the church. Guns were fired and bonfires lit. Peasants poured in to join the dancing.

The two brides, together with their attendants, were sumptuously attired by a team of seamstresses working under Madame Bérard, the barber's wife, who traveled up to Paris to check out the latest fashions. The top tailors, glovers, milliners, and shoemakers of Toulouse, suppressing painful memories of the earlier Daurignac fiasco, toiled over Thérèse's wedding outfits. The Bérards' bill alone came to nearly five thousand francs (enough to rent a luxury apartment in Paris for a year). None of these accounts was ever paid. But, over the next two decades and more, the local shopkeepers came to congratulate themselves on having launched Thérèse in style with a splendor that matched the scale of her subsequent operations on the national stage. Even after her downfall, her sheer nerve inspired a certain perverse pride. As an old man, the barber recounted with something like awe the story of how, on the day she was to leave for her honeymoon, Thérèse arranged to meet him on the station platform as she and her bridegroom boarded the midnight train for Paris so that the entire reckoning could be settled, instead of which he found himself, to his stupefaction, paying off her cabdriver:

"Can you believe that I was to pay for her cab—that she'd been driving about in it since the morning—and that it would cost me a mere twenty francs, which I was to add to my account! The twenty francs are still outstanding, incidentally. So that is how—as if it wasn't enough to have dressed her for the wedding—I ended up paying her cab fare as well!"

❧❧

The Humbert weddings puzzled people at the time and afterward. Contemporaries wondered what on earth could have persuaded an outstanding politician, clearly destined for the highest office, to marry off his two underage children to a couple of rascally young scroungers like the Daurignacs. The answer seemed to be the Château de Marcotte. Thérèse's fantasies, like her father's, drew strength from reality's shortcomings. When the real world fell to pieces around her ears, she took refuge in her dream castles, which never let her down. Marcotte's marble terraces and orange groves made up for the hard beds and meager diet in the dismal attics of the rue de Taur. Thérèse liked to think that the property had been left her by one of the kindly spinster aunts who peopled her imagination. She gave this testator different names at different times to different people. It might have been a Mademoiselle Lagourdère, or a Mademoiselle Latrémollière, or then again a Mademoiselle Baylac with usufruct to Mademoiselle Lucas.

There can be no doubt that on some level Thérèse persuaded herself, and perhaps her husband too, that Marcotte genuinely existed. As a student writing home to his mother, Frédéric described baskets of flowers and parcels of game arriving from his fiancée's estate. "At the time of my marriage," said Thérèse, "I believed so completely in Marcotte that we drew up an official power of attorney appointing Monsieur Parayre to run the property." Armand Parayre (who confirmed that he had indeed been named steward of Marcotte) was an eminently practical idealist with no time for fantasy. Determined to devote his life to the great reforming causes that fired his whole generation in France, he had given up any prospect of a more lucrative career in order to help liberate the illiterate masses through education. In his forties he would become a crusading newspaper editor, campaigning for progress, democracy, and the secularization of the state. No one who met him ever doubted his transparent honesty. Marcotte's authenticity could have found no better guarantee than the fact that a man of such unimpeachable integrity was prepared to vouch for it.

Parayre for his part accepted the purely honorary stewardship of a place neither he nor anyone else ever set eyes on because it was in the gift of Senator Humbert. The post was a sign of favor from a national figure who, for young radicals like Parayre, embodied the loftiest aspirations of the nascent Third Republic.

Humbert had impeccable credentials. His father had taken part in the French Revolution of 1789, and he himself had manned the barricades as a young man defending the republican tradition when street fighting broke out again in 1848. In Toulouse in the 1870s he attracted a band of ardent youths who looked to him for leadership in the ongoing struggle against reaction. They included

Armand Parayre, the idealistic young village
schoolmaster who married Catherine Fuzié,
going on to become a radical newspaper editor
and key figure in the Humbert empire in Paris.
(Collection Gaetana Matisse)

Parayre and his brothers, young Frédéric with his
Daurignac cousins, and the son of another university law professor, Arthur Huc, himself a distinguished future journalist in the proud left-wing tradition of the town. All of them were socialists,

free-thinkers, and Freemasons: passionate believers in the republican ideals that came under increasing threat toward the end of the century from the resurgent right wing. Parayre and his contemporaries longed to unite once more beneath the Revolution's proud banner of Liberté, Egalité, Fraternité. They marched, as France's top Freemason put it, "in the vanguard of the armies of progress" with good old Papa Humbert at their head.

But, if the senator was to become a power in the land by taking his rightful place among the new republican elite, he would need to keep up a certain state. Humbert had no money of his own (his father had been a small wine merchant in Metz before the German army seized Alsace-Lorraine from France). Even the noblest and most disinterested political program needs financing, and a daughter-in-law with a substantial dowry offered a possible way of doing it. Thérèse's detractors at the end of her career cast her as a scheming trickster who had invented a fraudulent inheritance expressly in order to trap the unsuspecting Frédéric and his rather more sagacious father. Frédéric's own mother threw her considerable weight behind this view, vigorously denouncing her niece as "the wretch who stole my son" (the two women had a history of mutual dislike, presumably going back to the fact that each knew too much about the other's origins for comfort). By this time Senator Humbert had died, passing into legend as a republican secular saint. Few cared to scrutinize his past too closely or to pick holes in the case for his defense put up by his doughty widow.

But people in Toulouse remembered the senator sounding out potential backers about the prospect of raising money in advance on his daughter-in-law's estate. Within a few years of the marriage, Humbert personally arranged to mortgage Marcotte on the strength of three bonds—testifying apparently to a value of 780,000 francs—which Thérèse fished out of her bodice at his signal in the presence of four witnesses (including the lawyer who later described the scene in court). Marcotte was not the only deal Humbert brokered for Thérèse. He was equally involved with another nonexistent estate, this time a plantation of cork oaks in Portugal, with a history very similar to Marcotte's.

Louis Daurignac remembered talk of his sister's Portuguese inheritance even before the family left Aussonne. He thought the property came from Thérèse's old schoolmistress in Rabastens. Others believed it had been left her by a Portuguese friend of her mother's: a passerby who had collapsed with a heart attack in the rue de Pomme, breaking Madame Daurignac's glass shopwindow. When she nursed him back to health, he repaid her with a legacy to her little daughter (who was also perhaps his own). In 1874—the year the Daurignacs lost everything—a Senhor R. A. died in Lisbon, according to Thérèse, leaving his estate to her. She said she had heard the news from the Portuguese consul in Toulouse. From then on she kept the title deeds stuffed in her blouse, but her fellow citizens remained unimpressed, and the possibility of obtaining a mortgage in the estate of Sabatou-Blancou never got off the ground. It would be another eight years before the Portuguese property brought in a serious sum.

Senator Humbert had achieved the summit of his ambition in January of that year, when he was appointed keeper of the seals, or minister of justice. He had finally become a prince of the new republican aristocracy. The first business acquaintance to whom he mentioned his daughter-in-law's Portuguese inheritance—a Doctor Fourès of Coursan, near Narbonne, in the southwest of France—leaped at the chance to advance him sixty thousand francs (the rough equivalent of $200,000 today). It would have been absurd at the time to question the good faith of a man who had just been appointed to the highest legal office in the land. But twenty years later, almost a decade after Humbert's death, when a police search failed to locate either Marcotte or Sabatou-Blancou, doubts crept in. Humbert was a shrewd negotiator celebrated throughout France for his grasp of legal strategy and tactics. Even supposing that the brain that wrote the constitution of the Third Republic could initially have been fooled by an unsophisticated girl with no legal background whatsoever, it was hard to credit that the minister could have gone on being her dupe.

Nobody apparently realized, then or later, that the two were uncle and niece. Once they had left Toulouse, both parties studiously concealed their relationship. Neither Thérèse nor any of the Humberts ever admitted that she and her husband were first cousins, or that the minister of justice had known her from the days when he lived in lodgings above her mother's shop. Over the years he had seen Thérèse develop from a child with a talent for artless make-believe into a performer who could virtually hypnotize hardheaded shopkeepers like Bérard. "What gave her her power was her astonishing fertility of invention," the barber himself explained in retrospect,

> and above all her staggering, superlative audacity! She would ask you the most preposterous favors in such a natural way that you accepted them as natural too, and never realized you'd been had until it was too late. She played some shocking tricks on me, even when I thought I knew her well.

Thérèse's creative gift was spontaneous and natural. "She lied as a bird sings," said a witness who knew her in her prime. She combined the psychological subtlety of an experienced actor with a novelist's narrative exuberance. If she had chosen books, instead of real life, as the medium for her romantic fictions about missing deeds, locked coffers, surprise legacies, and long-lost parents, she would have been a nineteenth-century bestseller. There was nothing calculating to start with about her absurd, implausible, and hopelessly inconsistent fabrications. It was only gradually that the dream castles described in such loving circumstantial detail were replaced by relatively prosaic but portable, easily concealable (and eminently forgeable) bearer bonds. The plot was skillfully streamlined, and the multiple, hydra-headed, perpetually changing benefactors narrowed down to one. The process took place in the five years following Thérèse's marriage, which were also the five years in which her Uncle Humbert played for the highest stakes of his career.

❧❧❧

The senator was said to have been the first to give the unlikely name of Crawford to his daughter-in-law's Portuguese well-wisher. In Thérèse's own

The CRAWFRAUD INHERITANCE, or The Secrets of a Strongbox: one of many cartoons depicting the opening of the strongbox said to contain Thérèse's Crawford legacy. *(Bibliothèque des Arts Décoratifs, Paris, all rights reserved; photo: © Jean-Loup Charmet, Paris)*

version, Crawford was an English milord who happened to fall ill in the very lodging house where she was living in Toulouse. Like her mother before her, she tended this passing stranger on his sickbed in the rue de Taur, where he eventually died, but not before drawing up a will in his nurse's favor. This will was inscribed on a marble slab inlaid in Crawford's bedroom wall: a virtuoso touch that got Thérèse into such trouble with troublesome customers who wanted to walk up and inspect the wall that Milord's death had to be relocated three hundred miles eastward to Nice.

Thérèse told this story to all comers, adding "with a stammer and tears in her eyes that her mother had enjoyed a very close relationship with the man who had just died, making her his heir." It was characteristic of Thérèse's new and worldlier approach that Crawford was now clearly understood to have been her mother's lover, with the implication that she herself was his natural daughter. Signs of her old careless, prodigal inventiveness surfaced in a story she told Catherine Parayre, about how the Daurignacs had once rescued a child from the clutches of a kidnapper at the Pyrenean resort of Bagnères-de-Bigorre (or could it have been Bagnères-de-Luchon?), where the colossally rich and lavish Crawford happened to be staying. In yet another variation Crawford was an American whose life she saved after an accident in what must have been a phenomenally early motor car. Details from these and other experimental drafts fed into the final master text, which featured an American millionaire called Robert Henry Crawford, who died at Nice on September 7, 1877 (a year to the day before the Beauzelle weddings), having signed the usual will the day before, naming Thérèse as sole beneficiary. This last and best of all her benefactors left her a princely one hundred million francs (about a third of a billion dollars today).

"What demonstrates above all else the genius of Thérèse," wrote an old friend (who only ever identified herself as "Madame X"),

> is the grandeur, the sheer immensity of the scale on which she operated. If she had laid claim to an inheritance of no more than four or six million, she would not have lasted two years, and would with difficulty have managed to raise a miserable few thousand francs. But a *hundred million*! People took their hats off to a sum like that as they would have done before the Pyramid of Cheops, and their admiration prevented them from seeing straight.

Cartoon showing the imaginary Crawford family gathered
for the reading of the will. *(Bibliothèque des Arts Décoratifs,
Paris, all rights reserved; photo: © Jean-Loup Charmet, Paris)*

Scale, simplicity, and orderly arrangement were central to the story that emerged, once Thérèse's rampant fantasies had been edited and authorized by the combined legal intelligence of the Humberts, father and son. The two were said to have spent weeks or even months together in the summer of 1883, holed up in a country retreat outside Paris, refining the details of a scheme that was already well on the way to a radical repackaging of the family's finances.

The change came none too soon for the young Humberts, who had spent their first two years of married life in Paris at 68, rue Monge among the squalid cafés, cheap wineshops, and fly-by-night lodging houses of the Latin Quarter. They survived from hand to mouth on heavy borrowings, heavier debts, and occasional handouts from Frédéric's father. Thérèse was used to dodging duns and bamboozling bailiffs with court orders, but her husband had to learn from scratch. When Thérèse became pregnant, her two younger sisters came up from Toulouse to camp out in the attics of the rue Monge with their aged father. Auguste Daurignac—or d'Aurignac as he now liked to be known—was in his eightieth year in 1880, when his daughter presented him with his first grandchildren, twin babies, one of whom died at birth. The family moved that year with the survivor, a girl called Eve, into better lodgings near the Opéra on the Chaussée d'Antin.

The young Humberts' upward mobility accelerated into top gear with Frédéric's father's nomination, on January 30, 1882, as justice minister in the cabinet formed by Charles Freycinet after the fall of Léon Gambetta. They bought a whole house, or *hôtel particulier,* that January, on the rue Fortuny, behind the fashionable Parc Monceau, where they kept four servants as well as a carriage and horses of their own. Two months later they acquired an even grander country residence near Melun, in the forest of Fontainebleau, fifteen miles south of Paris. The Château de Vives-Eaux was the first of Thérèse's real-life dream castles: a mock-Gothic pile set in a wooded park above a series of pools on the lawns below the house, descending to a private lake linked by a broad channel to the Seine.

❧❧❧

Frédéric was by now installed as his father's principal private secretary, or *chef de cabinet*. Emile Daurignac and Armand Parayre came up to Paris with their families to join the new minister's train. Political dinners at the *hôtel* in the rue Fortuny, and weekend house parties at Vives-Eaux, were organized by Armand's wife, Catherine, and hosted by Frédéric's wife, Thérèse. These were the performances for which they had rehearsed as girls at village hops and country dances in Aussonne. Thérèse adapted effortlessly to the social showmanship and conspicuous consumption of the Parisian Belle Epoque, easily eclipsing her sober middle-aged aunt Humbert and her retiring cousin Alice (who was her sister-in-law twice over), in the role of the minister's unofficial hostess. She set herself to woo the cream of republican high society just as she had once bewitched the farmers of Haute-Garonne. Young Madame Humbert, with her breathy voice, her Toulouse accent, and her charming little lisp, proved a credit to her father-in-law. Even the most supercilious Parisians were

Frédéric Humbert as *chef de cabinet* in the Ministry of
Justice: The sharp legal brain of Thérèse's shy and self-
effacing husband smoothed her path behind the scenes.
(Photo: © Topham Picturepoint)

beguiled by the freshness of her frankly rustic manners, and by her air of longing to learn what they had to say. They were still more intrigued by the piquant rumors beginning to circulate about her supposedly fabulous wealth.

If the story of Thérèse's inheritance needed to be tried out in many different drafts before it could be established on a sound business footing as a money-making concern, so did the practical machinery. At the beginning of 1883, the young Humberts traveled south, staying at the best hotel in Narbonne with a retinue of courtiers and attendants. Word got around that rich pickings were to be had. The great heiress with her ministerial connections in Paris was courted by eager lawyers, speculative financiers, land agents, and landowners only too anxious to lend money or, alternatively, sell off their assets. The Crédit Foncier chipped in with nine hundred thousand francs. Other banks and businesses between them advanced as much again.

The Humberts now disposed of capital on a scale previously unimaginable by anyone except perhaps Thérèse. She herself had made a triumphal return to Toulouse the year before, in order to deposit sixty thousand francs with the Banque de France, announcing that it was the revenue from her Portuguese cork oaks. Even her great expectations had grown by leaps and bounds since then. "The inheritance inflated in front of your eyes, it mounted up into the millions," said a witness, describing good old Papa Humbert's method of bidding up advances on a legacy that had started out at no more than a paltry few hundred thousand francs. "It was no longer an inheritance. It was a geometrical progression."

❧❦❧

The main business of the visit to Narbonne made all previous transactions look small. The Humberts spent months negotiating the purchase of the Château de Celeyran, the ancestral home of the Comtesse de Toulouse-Lautrec (whose son Henri, painting landscapes at Celeyran that summer, would shortly galvanize Montmartre with his eye-catching posters of raunchy cabaret stars). Celeyran changed hands on March 29, 1883, for two million francs, a sum that made people's eyes grow wide. All of it was borrowed. A Monsieur Bagnères lent 1.6 million francs (which the Humberts would repay only after years of lawyers' threats, judicial writs, bailiffs' raids, and a final lawsuit). The estate was to be mortgaged and stripped of its assets, including the fine wines from its vineyards (bottled and sold from now on by the Humberts' wine merchant in Melun). None of the family ever lived there. The property was managed first by Armand Parayre's brother-in-law, Jacques Boutiq, and later by his brother, Alexandre Parayre. Its prime importance was as an advertising investment which boosted the Humberts' credit, bringing in handsome profits from lenders throughout their native region.

The Narbonne spending spree set a pattern that would serve the Humberts well for the next two decades. Spectacular display, speedy exploitation, and colossal turnover were their watchwords. One of many puzzles, for those who tried to analyze the workings of the scheme in retrospect, was its initial funding. Start-up capital—enough to set up the establishment on the rue Fortuny, and make the first confidence-building bank deposits—must have come from somewhere. The answer once again lay with Justice Minister Humbert. His first move on taking office had been to supervise the winding up of the Union Générale Bank, which had collapsed, causing panic on European stock markets in January 1882. Shares had been virtually wiped out by January 30, when Humbert put the bank's affairs in the hands of the public prosecutor, who promptly arrested its founder, Eugène Bontoux. The bank was declared bankrupt three days later, ruining thousands of investors (including the great pioneering art dealer, Paul Durand-Ruel, who had been for many years the impressionists' only backer).

The Union Générale was a speculative venture, set up expressly to undermine the Rothschild Bank (which helped the government resolve the stock market crisis by massive transfers of capital). Funds came from the anti-Semitic, pro-Catholic, royalist right wing, rallying behind what looked like a vigorous new thrust in the campaign to topple the still young and shaky Third Republic. The Union Générale's failure was hailed as a public triumph for Humbert, for the Rothschilds, and for the republican cause in general. But shortly after the crash, the new minister secretly deposited large sums (some said as much as two million francs) in various private accounts. One of them was with the Comptoir d'Alsace, whose director, Léopold Sée, saw this windfall as a payoff from the Rothschilds. Sée and others maintained that Thérèse Humbert had supplied a timely alibi for her father-in-law's otherwise inexplicable access of capital.

Although Humbert lost his ministry with the fall of Freycinet's cabinet in July 1883, the family fortunes continued to rise. The former minister retired to Vives-Eaux, saying he meant to sort out his daughter-in-law's inheritance ("I'm going to have my work cut out clearing up the death duties"). At the beginning of the summer the legacy in question was reported to be 1.5 million francs from Thérèse's Le Havre godmother. By the time Humbert left Vives-Eaux to return to Paris, the testator's identity had changed, and the sum had multiplied more than sixtyfold into the Crawford millions.

That autumn the young Humberts bought a newspaper: *L'Avenir de Seine et Marne,* which Armand Parayre would run for the next decade as a rip-roaring radical organ, laying into all enemies of progress and masterminding Frédéric's election as the republican deputy for Melun. In 1884 two more estates near Melun, Orsonville and Villiers-en-Bière, were added to the Humbert portfolio. The year after that Thérèse gave a housewarming party, marked by what even hardened Parisians saw as unheard-of luxury, to celebrate her family's final move into the most splendid of all the properties she ever owned, at 65, avenue de la Grande Armée.

The avenue de la Grande Armée was a continuation of the Champs-Elysées, running westward from the Arc de Triomphe through the cliffs and ravines of monolithic apartment buildings put up to house the new men—bankers, entrepreneurs, speculative developers—who were the architects of modern Paris. Baron Haussmann's scheme for urban renewal meant tearing down whole districts of the capital to make way for spacious vistas along broad avenues lined with imposing, even futuristic buildings. Paris in the closing decades of the nineteenth century saw an explosion of energy and confidence in some ways comparable to what would happen in the United

The mansion at 65, avenue de la Grande Armée
where Thérèse made her dreams come true.
(Photo: © Topham Picturepoint)

States in the 1920s. Industrialists who built railroads, mechanized production, and pioneered the first department stores turned the old social, financial, and cultural certainties upside down. Innovation and experiment were at a premium. New money backed new ideas, whether it meant installing gas lighting, astounding passersby with the latest iron-framed glass architecture, or buying the impressionist paintings that scandalized less forward-looking contemporaries. The reforming vision of the Third Republic went hand in hand with capital expansion, rich returns on rash investment, and a thirst for novelty that made Paris fashions the envy of the world.

No one exemplified the twin goals of this new world—democratic progress and prodigal display—more exuberantly than young Madame Humbert. She was not yet out of her twenties when she finally moved with her family into the castle of her dreams in 1885. Her very naïveté was as crucial as her persuasive powers to the smooth working of her father-in-law's scheme. If investors were to gain confidence in this particular illusion, Thérèse must indulge to the full all the cravings suppressed but not stifled by her penurious past.

She embodied not only her own but other people's dreams. Like a 1920s Hollywood movie star, she aimed to make the public gasp at the sumptuous extravagance of her lifestyle.

Thérèse's new house on the avenue de la Grande Armée was known in the Humberts' circle as "the Château." Its massive portals opened onto vestibules, antechambers, and a waiting room furnished with antique guns and musical instruments, where visitors waited to be summoned before climbing the marble staircase to the palatial apartments on the second floor: the billiard room, the dining room, and the great studio, or salon, stuffed with silk upholstery, fine old carvings, Gothic sideboards, bronzes, silverware, and cloisonné enamels. In these gilded halls, hung with priceless tapestries and furnished with Renaissance thrones and chests, Thérèse could at last play out her childhood scenario of a world richer, grander, more clear-cut and more highly charged than anything real life had to offer.

"Anyone who was anyone in politics, at the bar, in the courts, the government, and the world of high finance ended up at the Humberts' house," wrote Madame X, who went there herself most days. Three successive presidents of the republic, and at least five prime ministers, were Madame Humbert's personal friends. The populist hero General Boulanger made her house his second home, in his heyday regularly arriving with a train of hangers-on headed by his majordomo. In the mid-1890s President Casimir-Pierre Périer himself presided over one end of Madame Humbert's dining table with Henri du Buit, the leader of the Paris bar, seated at the other. Archbishops, ambassadors, bankers, cabinet ministers, dukes, and diplomats attended her parties and receptions. Her box at the Opéra was crammed. Her guest lists appeared in the next morning's papers. Lines of carriages filled the broad street before her door.

Her short, upright, already thickening, and stoutly upholstered figure took on a semiregal bearing. She favored high-piled, crownlike hats, surmounted by rearing confections of fruit, birds' nests, or peacock feathers. Madame Humbert's headgear and the costumes that went with it made all Paris stare, not always sympathetically ("she looked like a reliquary, stuck all over with jewels," Madame X wrote tartly). The capital's finest jew-

La Grande Thérèse, with her husband and only daughter,
in one of the hats that made all Paris gasp.
(Photo: © Jean-Loup Charmet, Paris)

elers competed to satisfy her passion for precious stones, sending around on approval the bags of diamonds, emeralds, and sapphires she had longed for as a girl. Her dresses came from Jacques Doucet or the Maison Worth (in a single year she ran up bills with each of 97,000 and 32,000 francs, respectively).

❦

Thérèse was staging the performance of her life, and it was essential to the success of the whole production that she herself, her house, and everything in it—including the guests—should be of first-class quality. She knew the top people, and was dressed by the most sought-after couturiers and modistes. She patronized the best antiquarians, the most fashionable decorators, and the ritziest picture dealer (Georges Petit, the man who made a fortune out of the impressionists after Durand-Ruel lost everything to the Union Générale Bank).

But Thérèse never felt entirely at ease with anyone except her extended family—brothers, sisters, Toulouse trusties—who knew that the whole enchanted castle was a game of make-believe. She depended absolutely on the clan (*la tribu*), which had followed her to Paris from her hometown, where all of them had begun by sitting at the feet of good old Papa Humbert. Chief among them was the inconspicuous Frédéric, who gave up politics after a few years to dabble in the arts instead, writing playlets, publishing a slim volume of verse, taking painting lessons from one of the leading Salon practitioners of the day, Ferdinand Roybet. Frédéric's role was to oversee the smooth working of the scheme set up by his father, and he played it in private with admirable efficiency. In public the world wrote him off as a weakling, wholly under his wife's thumb. Certainly he seems never to have looked at another woman, and Thérèse, unexpectedly prudish when it came to marital infidelity, loudly proclaimed her devotion to him. Her imagination shied away from sexual involvement: She got her kicks from a different kind of power.

Emotional support came from her old confi-
dante, Catherine Parayre. As Thérèse's second-in-
command, Madame Parayre ran the household with
a staff of twenty under her, and a budget of two hundred thousand francs a year. She made a formidable
chatelaine, straight backed, stiff necked, and tight
lipped, inspiring terror in all those who tried and
failed to gain entrance to 65, avenue de la Grande
Armée. Next in order of importance was Romain
Daurignac, who dealt with new arrivals (apart from
guest celebrities) once they had gotten past the
dragon at the door. Romain was the joker of the
family. Short, dark, and handsome, black-mus-
tached, a smooth talker with a flair for witty one-
liners, he traveled all over France on his sister's business and kept a girl in every town. But he also had a
darker side. If Frédéric was the brains of the production, Madame Parayre the house manager, and
Thérèse the undoubted star, Romain was in charge
backstage, where unseen strings were pulled, levers
operated, and traps sprung. He had his own quarters
in a wing behind the house, with a separate entrance
opening on the rue Pergolèse, next to the coach
house, yard, and stables at the back.

His brother Emile—solid, bearded, looking older than his thirty years—lent respectability to the outfit. He lived out, sharing a comparatively modest apartment in the rue de Rivoli with his wife, two small children, and his elderly parents-in-law. Gustave Humbert had been appointed vice president of the Senate after he left the Ministry of Justice, becoming a high court judge in 1889, and Chief Justice of the Cour des Comptes (Audit Office) the year after. Venerable and venerated, loaded with honors by a grateful nation, he gave the family enterprise not only legal expertise, but the priceless asset of his great name and reputation.

The three elder Daurignac siblings had always operated as a unit to which the next two—Louis and Marie-Louise—never quite belonged. As children they were too young, and as adults, too recalcitrant. Louis, who had rejected Thérèse's plan for him to join the Trappists, was generally agreed to be the only honest Daurignac. He would have nothing to do with his sister's stage machinery, and she dealt with him as ruthlessly as she treated anything that bugged her: by banishing him, her, or it, physically or mentally, and going on as if there had never been a problem. In Louis's case she simply bought a colonial property in Tunisia and shipped him out to run it. A similar fate awaited Marie-Louise, who had defied Thérèse from infancy. A marriage was arranged with Frédéric's cousin Lucien Humbert, who was packed off to become French consul in the Caucasus, where he caught cholera and died, leaving his widow with two small children to support.

Maria, the youngest and most docile of the Daurignacs, had always been Thérèse's pet. She had none of her eldest sister's fire or bite, and she was no great beauty either. But she was slim, willowy, and gentle, with the added attraction of being some sort of heiress in her own right. Thérèse had seen to it from their beginnings in Aussonne (when Maria was said to have come in for a tidy sum under the *curé*'s will) that the occasional minor legacy had her little sister's name on it. Maria had a gift for shy and graceful improvisation, which Thérèse encouraged. Her own daughter, Eve, was still too small, and temperamentally too close to her father, to show much promise in this line. Maria's pliancy made her readily accept direction, but she was enough of a Daurignac to enjoy embroidering her part once she had learned the lines. She became the adoptive daughter of the house, a Humbert princess to be wooed and won by what a contemporary observer called "the

Thérèse's sister, Maria Daurignac, a princess of the house of Humbert wooed by the young and thrusting dauphins of the Third Republic.
(Photo: © Hulton Getty, London)

dauphins of the Third Republic." Over the years it sometimes seemed that half the young hopefuls at the Paris bar were suitors for Maria's hand.

❧✦❧

Old Father Daurignac, who had been well into his sixties when his youngest child was born, lived just long enough to see the fulfillment of his own and his firstborn's wildest dreams. When the Comte d'Aurignac—for he had finally ennobled himself—died in 1886, the pomp and splendor of his end equaled the wretchedness of his birth eighty-five years earlier. He lay in state in his daughter's house, and was borne round the corner for a solemn funeral at the gleaming, gold-encrusted society church of St.-Honoré d'Eylau. A fantasist to the last, he had made such a drama out of the provisions in his will that, on the night he died, Armand Parayre had to be summoned to mount guard with his revolver over the family safe.

❧✦❧

his legendary strongbox, shrouded in mystery like all the Daurignacs' ancestral coffers, held the secret at the heart of the great house on the avenue de la Grande Armée. In it lay Crawford's fabled hundred million francs in bearer bonds. It occupied its own locked chamber on the third floor, which no one but Monsieur or Madame Humbert ever entered (except for Madame Parayre, who cleaned and polished the strongbox once a week). Every so often a favored visitor—generally an inquisitive or exacting lawyer—might be permitted to peep around the door. More rarely, the safe would be opened just long enough for a major creditor to gaze in respectful silence at the bulky packets filled with the sealed envelopes that contained the hidden treasure. On more than one occasion the family's most faithful agent—Maître Dumort, a prominent provincial solicitor from Rouen—was smuggled into the next room so that he could watch through a crack as Frédéric Humbert and Romain Daurignac undid the wrappings to clip the annual coupons off the bearer bonds.

Each summer, when the family left for vaca-

tion at Vives-Eaux, the packets would be trans-
ferred to a valise that was brought downstairs
before the assembled household and ritually pad-
locked for the journey to Armand Parayre's wrist.
Parayre's loyalty to the justice minister never fal-
tered. Having once identified the new dawn of
republican idealism with the Humberts' cause, he
served both with the unconditional devotion of a
proud and generous nature. Small, wiry, dark
haired, and olive skinned, he was apt to catch fire
in a blaze of enthusiasm or indignation. He was a
pugilist as well as a crack shot, quick on the draw,
and skilled in the arts of self-defense. In 1885 he
fought and won a duel over press freedom with a
rival journalist in Melun. Whenever the honor of
the Humberts was at stake, Parayre was the man
they sent for to retrieve it.

❧❧

But beneath all the charades, the castle rituals,
and ceremonies lay an uglier reality. The Humberts'
state apartments gave way at the back to a warren of
little rooms, offices, and cells presided over by

Romain. He had been brought up, like his siblings, on Thérèse's stories, but the aspect that appealed to him was not so much their sumptuosity and spectacle as their seamy underside. Romain had a taste for thuggery. He flourished in an atmosphere heavy with menace, secrecy, and violence. He had his lair on the far side of a door concealed in the wall of the great staircase. Lawyers met in these back parts. Angry lenders were fobbed off, tradesmen milked and bilked. "This was the field on which every sort of battle was fought out with infuriated creditors and vengeful suppliers," wrote F. I. Mouthon, the investigative journalist who came in the end to understand the Humberts better than any other contemporary observer. "Romain did not always emerge unscathed from these rough confrontations with marauding passions."

Once he was discovered bleeding on the floor after a fight with Armand's brother, Alexandre, the steward of Celeyran, whose wages had not been paid. Another time the frantic wife of a ruined newspaper proprietor from Melun drew a revolver on Thérèse, whose life was saved only by Romain's deflecting the gunshots through the

The ladykiller Romain Daurignac: Thérèse's
brother, whose taste for thuggery and violence
underpinned the Humbert empire.
(Photo: © Hulton Getty, London)

window. The first of these incidents was hushed up ("Romain wound himself in bandages, put up with the pain, and held his tongue"). But the police were called to arrest the unfortunate lady, who spent the better part of the next two years shut up in a Swiss lunatic asylum. The celebrated head of the Paris police force, Louis Lépine, was a devoted friend of Madame Humbert, and the superintendent at the local station—a certain Commissaire Wagram—could be relied on to support the family in affairs like this one.

The number of dissatisfied, often dangerous, sometimes almost unhinged customers demanding their money back increased each year as the workings of the Humberts' scheme screwed down more and more tightly on its victims. Whatever its cost in human misery and despair, the machinery was, technically and legally, elegant in the extreme. Inside the strongbox with its cargo of forged bearer bonds lay four key documents. The first was Robert Henry Crawford's will, dated September 6, 1877, which named Thérèse as sole beneficiary. Next came a second will, signed on the same day, this time leaving everything to be divided equally between Maria Daurignac and the dying millionaire's two American nephews, Robert and Henry Crawford. The third document, dated March 1883, was an agreement by the Crawford brothers to hand over their uncle's entire fortune into Madame Humbert's keeping, on condition that it remain intact until the dispute had finally been settled (the Humberts were to live meanwhile on the annual interest from the bonds). Last was a deed, drawn up eighteen months later, under which the Crawfords consented to waive their claim altogether in return for six million francs in cash, together with Maria's hand in marriage for one or the other brother.

These four documents provided the hinge on which the whole scam turned. The claims of the Crawford nephews, which prevented Madame Humbert from ever actually laying hands on her rightful wealth, admirably explained her unending need for credit. When the Crawfords finally named their price for withdrawing from the field, lenders fell over themselves to supply the triumphant heiress with six million francs at advantageous rates of interest. Madame Humbert's story was that the dastardly Crawfords had refused to take her money, dishonoring their pledge on the pretext that Maria declined to become engaged to either of them. In October 1885 a case against the two brothers was brought before the Civil Tribunal of the Seine, which delivered its verdict a year later in Madame Humbert's favor.

❧❧❧

The Tribunal of the Seine was, of course, a real court just as the leading advocates hired to represent each side in this dispute were real lawyers. The Crawfords themselves did not exist, but no court was ever asked to pronounce on the validity of the two wills, or for that matter on the existence of the millions. The point at issue was whether or not the imaginary plaintiffs (neither of whom ever appeared in court) had reneged on their no less imaginary agreement of 1883. Once the court ruled that they had, the way lay open for proceedings that in theory never needed to end. The beauty of it was that *Humbert* v. *Crawford* litigation could—and did— drag on indefinitely, from appeal to counterappeal, tended by the grandest lawyers in the land, as the case rose slowly up through virtually every court in France.

Over the years the Crawfords were promoted from purely imaginary figments to phantoms haunting the Humberts' château, flitting from room to room, glimpsed around a door or through a peephole. From time to time they materialized unexpectedly elsewhere, in or outside Paris. In 1885 they were spotted by a bailiff who served papers on them in the Hôtel du Louvre. Later the same year one of them turned up to brief a barrister in Le Havre. An eyewitness reported an odd scene in which Gustave Humbert urged a tearful Maria Daurignac to give up her love for a flighty foreigner like Robert Crawford. Excitement regularly rose and fell, depending on whether the engagement was reported to be on or off. One evening, just as fifty people were sitting down to table at 65, avenue de la Grande Armée, an enormous Chinese vase was delivered with a fond message for Maria from her American suitor.

Suspense reached a peak with a dinner party billed beforehand as the occasion on which Maria

Humbert mania swept the Paris press when the scandal
eventually broke in 1902: Here Thérèse, with her elegant
younger sister Maria, is greeted by the trial judge disguised
as a cabaret host: "Well, Madame Humbert, have you any
news of the good Monsieur Crawfraud?" *(Bibliothèque des
Arts Décoratifs, Paris, all rights reserved; photo: © Jean-Loup
Charmet, Paris)*

would at last accept a marriage proposal from one or other of the young Crawfords. Maximum publicity surrounded this event, which promised to remove the final obstacle standing between Madame Humbert and her fortune. All Paris was agog. Invitations were fiercely coveted. On the night itself, twenty-five distinguished guests took their seats to watch the supposed Robert Crawford solemnly place a packet of jewels, including a gold ring, at Maria's place. She pushed his offering aside as if she had not seen it. At the end of the first course, he retrieved the ring and tried to place it on her finger. Maria flushed scarlet, thrust his arm away, and rose to her feet, holding all eyes riveted, before bursting into tears and running from the room. "The marriage will have to be postponed again," Madame Humbert announced glumly to her guests.

It was generally agreed in retrospect that Romain and Emile Daurignac must have impersonated the Crawford brothers, who spoke French with what their listeners assumed was an American accent. Neither ever said a memorable word, but the scenes in which they took part were so carefully stage-managed that no more was needed than a bare appearance. Conviction came from the authentic splendor of the setting, the genuine eminence of the guests, above all the presence of the former minister of justice. "His name, his titles and functions meant that he had the police, the courts, and the judicial tribunals in his pocket," wrote a contemporary, "and after his death, the republican prestige of so grand an ancestor went on providing his family with cover for many years." Humbert died at the age of seventy-two in 1894. His bust stood in the Hall of Honor of the Law Faculty at Toulouse University. His state portrait—painted by his son Frédéric, who won a medal for it at the Paris Salon—continued to preside in ermine over the château on the avenue de la Grande Armée.

It was years since Thérèse had taken over from him as director of her own affairs, but his restraining influence had supplied a sobering contact with reality. His death precipitated a series of showdowns, beginning with the liquidation of the Girard Bank, which had been one of the Humberts' major creditors. In February 1895 the bank's president, Paul Girard, called on Madame Humbert in a last desperate bid to persuade her to repay him. She refused, whereupon he pulled a gun and shot at her. When the bullet missed, Girard drove straight back to his office to shoot himself.

His name may not have been the first but it was certainly the most impressive on what Madame Humbert called her suicide register. A receiver called Duret was appointed to look into the affairs of the Girard Bank. The Humberts opened negotiations by trying to bribe him over a friendly dinner that ended in a fistfight with Romain, who called the police. Relations were temporarily patched up, but Duret never forgot or forgave this incident. In May the Humberts were publicly denounced for the first time as crooks by the right-wing scandal sheet, *Libre Parole*. Romain's response was to call in the spy ring he had built up for silencing dissatisfied creditors. "'We've got the man behind the press campaign," he told Duret, "and that will be the end of it, you'll see."

The Humberts' own paper, the republican *L'Avenir de Seine et Marne*, had been wound up with the minister's death the year before, leaving Armand Parayre out of a job. He had served his master faithfully for nearly two decades in return

for minimal expenses, drawing no salary and com-
mitting his own and his wife's savings to the
Humberts' cause. His two young daughters both
went out to work at this point. The elder, Amélie,
was taken on by her Aunt Nine, her mother's sister, Madame Boutiq, who ran a hat shop on one
of the grand boulevards in Paris. The younger,
Berthe, became a teacher, like her father, in a village
school just outside Toulouse. Still unemployed—
and possibly unemployable at fifty-one—their
father called at the Humberts' house, to ask for the
meager compensation on which they had agreed,
only to be shown the door with characteristic brutality by Romain. A scuffle and an exchange of
death threats developed into a full-scale duel. The
pair fought by English boxing rules at the insis-
tence of Parayre, who left his tormentor with a
bloody nose in spite of being the older of the two
by fourteen years. The police, summoned as usual
by Romain, proved less than cooperative, and no
charge was made.

Reinstated in the Humberts' favor, Parayre
sailed for Madagascar, where he hoped to bring
education to the local people. The island had been

overrun the year before by French colonial troops, and Parayre's outspoken criticism of army brutality led to his hasty recall. From the Humberts' point of view, he had at least been safely out of the country during the critical phase of legal proceedings brought against them by Duret on behalf of the Girard Bank. Things looked black for the Humberts during this affair, which took place at Elbeuf, in Normandy, in 1896, with an appeal hearing two years later. Duret had retained the barrister René Waldeck-Rousseau, Léon Gambetta's former associate, himself soon to become president of the republic. Rousseau described the Humbert inheritance in court as "the greatest swindle of the century," a phrase that would come back to haunt the perpetrators ever afterward. Their counsel was Thérèse's old friend Maître du Buit, a legal eagle universally respected "for the austerity of his morals, the sincerity of his republican convictions, his sternness as a barrister, the skill and eloquence of his pleas in court." Maître du Buit opened for the Humberts with the ringing declaration: "I stand before the tribunal armed with nothing but the naked Truth."

His clients survived this dual ordeal by the skin of their teeth with a settlement of two million francs to pay. Money had to be raised urgently on an unprecedented scale. Until now Humbert funds had come mainly from their native South. From the mid-1890s onward, the wealthy industrialists of the North were systematically targeted by lawyers operating out of Rouen and Lille. Many of these lawyers, highly respected in their own communities, entrusted their own personal fortunes to the Humberts' bottomless coffers. Maître Dumort of Rouen gave everything he had, a sum amounting in the end to well over 6 million francs (more like $19 million today). Maître Langlois, who drummed up 1.2 million francs from the Marquis de Cazeaux alone, claimed to have raised 12 million in all.

❧❧

Madame Humbert's reputation for offering the highest rates of interest in France was increasingly backed up by the undercover activities of her brother's hit men. Romain's propensity for extortion, blackmail, and physical force seems to have had free play after the minister's death. One of Dumort's clients—a major firm of distillers, Schotmann et fils of Lille—advanced 2 million francs in 1896. Three years later the murdered body of Paul Schotmann was discovered on a train from Douai to Lille. Rumor said that he had refused a further loan of 7 million francs (a sum duly handed over after his death by his brother, Jean, and his cousin, Emile Schotmann). Romain was never called to account for this murder, or for the subsequent death of a young nephew, his sister Marie-Louise's son Paul Humbert, who was found hanged after a mysterious raid on his parents' house. The family passed this death off as suicide, but many felt that Romain's violent instincts were once again running out of control.

If so, they were eventually reined in by Madame Humbert, whose taste ran to romantic or comic-opera scenarios rather than to her brother's deadly Grand Guignol. Even at the height of danger, with everything to play for, Thérèse relied on effrontery so bold that few had the nerve to call her bluff. One was the bailiff Quelquejay, cele-

C.I.D. agents toast the Crawfords at a police dinner
given by the Humberts with a chocolate replica of the
famous strongbox in the center of the table.

brated in legend ever afterward as the champion who came nearest to forcibly breaking open the strongbox. People talked in whispers of the day when Madame Humbert personally fought Quelquejay, disputing his papers check by check as she retreated step by step up the great staircase of 65, avenue de la Grande Armée, until sufficient funds arrived in the nick of time to pay him off. Another successful challenger was a minor moneylender who turned up at eight o'clock one morning, seeking repayment of the relatively trifling sum of 250,000 francs, and was put to wait with many others in the music room on the ground floor. "At midday he was still waiting," wrote Mouthon, describing the scene with relish:

> at one o'clock he demolished the piano; at two, he set about the harp and the military trophies; and, in spite of the intervention of Madame Parayre who brought him ten thousand francs from time to time, to calm his nerves and stave off his hunger pangs, he finally stuck his head out of the window with cries of "Stop thief!" and "Fire!" By five o'clock a crowd of a thousand people and

two fire engines had assembled in front of
the house. The troublemaker, satisfied with
a solid payment on account of one hundred
thousand francs, and in any case too smart
to risk an encounter with the police, calmly
made his escape by the rue Pergolèse, leaving Madame Parayre on the front doorstep,
still haranguing the crowd and the firemen.

For once Madame Humbert had met a
humorist capable of capping her jokes in her own
style. But most of her stooges had to make do with
payment in what a contemporary observer called
"the small change of hope." Any other sort of
change came from Madame Parayre's regular trips
to the pawnshop to cash in the week's offerings,
mainly from jewelers vying with one another for
Madame Humbert's trade. Once she commis-
sioned an elaborate pearl-and-diamond necklace,
to be made up at short notice for a friend, including as a mark of special favor jewels from the
imperial crown. These were hard to come by
(demand had outstripped supply in fashionable
circles from the moment the state put them on
sale), but the worried jeweler found his problem

Thérèse in her prime: "Ah, what a woman! No one
dared say anything to her, no one dared contradict her,
above all no one dared claim anything back from her!"
(*Photo © Jean-Loup Charmet, Paris*)

solved by a veiled lady who turned up in his shop next day, offering crown jewels for an exorbitant price in cash. The unknown lady was never seen again, and Madame Humbert's necklace was never paid for either. "Ah, what a woman!" said a Humbert employee, "no one dared say anything to her, no one dared caution her, above all no one dared claim anything back from her!"

La Grande Thérèse had emerged from the sticky patch that followed her father-in-law's death with her show firmly back on the road. After the dismissal of the first Girard appeal in 1898, and the silencing of fresh onslaughts in the right-wing press, she looked set for a long run. Critics who had grumbled openly at the beginning now fell silent. "What the Humberts wanted was to give themselves a theatrical décor," wrote Arthur Huc, the Toulouse journalist who had watched the production being tried out in its early stages: "The Humberts recruited more extras than accomplices."

✺✺✺

In the closing years of the nineteenth century, the Humbert show entered its magnificent last act. Art-world celebrities from Sarah Bernhardt to Emile Zola attended Thérèse's parties. The new president, Félix Faure, often dined at 65, avenue de la Grande Armée. The friends and families of his immediate predecessors—Périer and Sadi Carnot—still regularly visited Vives-Eaux for hunting parties in the forest or pleasure trips on the Seine in the Humberts' yacht. Supporters in the police force and the judiciary ranged from Maître du Buit and Police Chief Lépine to the Chief Justice of the Court of Appeals, Frédéric Périer. Madame Humbert could count on solidarity from the republican establishment, especially the upper echelons of Freemasonry, traditionally associated with the progressive Left in France.

One of her long-term backers was the attorney general, Maître Bulot, who had personally initiated the Daurignacs, Frédéric Humbert, and Armand Parayre as Freemasons in Toulouse almost a quarter of a century earlier. Radical Masons, roped in to support the cause by Parayre, included the hugely popular defense minister, Camille

Pelletan, and the rising young socialist star, Marcel Sembat. Madame Humbert's right-hand man—the nearest she ever came to an official lover or escort—was another Mason, Etienne Jacquin, secretary of the Légion d'Honneur, and chancellor of state at the Ministry of Justice. She traded favors at all levels, from the ministry to the humblest provincial town hall or courthouse. She could arrange for a disgraced magistrate or civil servant to be reinstated; for a prefect to be dismissed; for one creditor's son to be excused from military service, and another's to be pardoned for desertion. "Don't do that," a senior magistrate once said pleasantly to a witness who had threatened to denounce the Humberts. "Don't do that, or I shall be obliged to put you behind bars."

Madame Humbert's position—socially, politically, and from a business point of view—seemed impregnable. The unbeatable rates of interest she offered inspired confidence not only in major finance houses but in thousands of small investors, who had been persuaded to put their money into a new savings bank operating from Romain's back premises on the rue Pergolèse. The Rente Viagère

The Humberts at home. *From left*: Eve Humbert (daughter), Maître du Buit (advocate), Frédéric Humbert (*standing*), Maria Daurignac (*sitting*), Senator Barriere (*standing*), Madame Humbert (*sitting*).

(Photo: © Mary Evans Picture Library, London)

had been launched in 1893 on a wholly fraudulent base, with nonexistent capital and a glossy advertising brochure headed by pictures of the pope and President Paul Kruger of South Africa. Business prospered from the start. After three years the enterprise was handed over to Armand Parayre, who ran it as a genuine savings bank with such unexpected flair that, given another ten or twenty years, the Humberts would have been well on the way to becoming authentic millionaires.

Parayre celebrated his new job with a wedding party for his elder daughter, Amélie, who was married in January 1898 from 65, avenue de la Grande Armée. Her wedding dress came from Madame Humbert's own couturier, Maison Worth, and Monsieur Humbert signed the register as her witness together with his old colleague from the Ministry of Justice, Councillor of State Jacquin. Her dowry was a bag of jewels, a favorite Humbert wedding present for the children of old friends and supporters. Amélie used hers to buy a year's freedom for herself and her new husband, who was a penniless young painter called Henri Matisse. History does not relate what the Humberts made, if anything, of the strange, brightly colored, increasingly shocking modernistic paintings produced over the next decade and more by the man who married their housekeeper's daughter.

Frédéric Humbert for his part filled the picture gallery on the avenue de la Grande Armée with a very different type of picture, mostly gilt-edged Salon favorites with a sprinkling of old masters. He acquired paintings for the same reason that his wife collected precious stones. "The décor that surrounded the Humberts was designed to produce an illusion for potential clients as well as dazzling their guests," wrote the essayist Jules Claretie:

> The possession of a picture gallery in Paris . . . is an excellent way of establishing your credit. . . . Your standing goes up—like a quotation on the stock exchange—as soon as you put in a bid for a particular canvas. . . . Buying pictures can also be a sound moral investment.

As an index of creditworthiness, Frédéric Humbert's taste could hardly have been more reassuring: Raphael, Delacroix, Corot, and Courbet headed a solid phalanx of now-forgotten society painters—Isabey, Gervex, Baron Gérard—whose prices set new records in their day.

Many of them specialized in history painting, generally felt by nineteenth-century connoisseurs to be the highest form yet achieved by Western art. Humbert was no slouch at it himself, taking a gold medal in 1900 with his *Louis XIII and Mademoiselle de Hautefort* (which was snapped up by the duke of Marlborough, Winston Churchill's cousin, for Blenheim Palace in England). His studio cupboards were stocked with swords, shields, suits of armor, and elaborate medieval costumes for the models. He had set himself up with a luxury bachelor apartment in a studio building on the Place Vintimille, in one of the more sought-after artistic quarters of Paris, where he passed as a painter called Henri Lelong. This was by no means his only false identity. As a student he had signed his articles "Frédéric Haston," and in 1901 he published a slim volume of verse under the name "François Haussy."

Frédéric Humbert as a would-be Salon artist in
the luxuriously equipped studio where he turned out
fashionable history paintings.
(Photo: © Jean-Loup Charmet, Paris)

Dressing up, playacting, and impersonation had been a way of life in the Humbert household for so long that even the inmates must sometimes have found it hard to tell what was make-believe and what wasn't. Conspirators regularly disappeared through the concealed door on the grand staircase into Romain's secret lair. Raised voices, slammed doors, and the sound of fistfights or revolver shots gave everyday life an atmosphere more like that of adventure fiction. On one level the real Daurignac brothers played the nonexistent Crawfords. On another Thérèse coached her sister Maria in artificial scenes staged for the benefit of creditors. On a third Frédéric put on a play of his own about a medieval knight who falls in love with a beautiful princess on his way back from the Crusades. The piece was directed by a hired professional and performed in the picture gallery before a fashionable audience. The hero was played by the Humberts' only daughter, Eve, showing off her slender figure in a Crusader's shining armor, with her dashing Uncle Romain cast as a troubadour from Toulouse.

❦

The turn of the century saw a crescendo of theatrical activity as well as unparalleled ostentation in a household where even the lavatory brushes wore pink satin bows (the bows were purple in Frédéric's studio apartment). But all was not well behind the facade. The strain of keeping up appearances was beginning to tell on the Humberts. "They survived from one day to the next," wrote Arthur Huc, "always in search of fresh credit to clear yesterday's loan, struggling to raise money for the usurer as much as for themselves, reaping little or no benefit from their villainy." Even Thérèse's ingenuity came close to being overstretched. Cornered one day by an importunate dun who turned up with a posse of supporters, she turned at bay, crying, "Take that!" and ripping the necklace from her throat with such force that the string broke, scattering pearls across the floor. The whole household fell to its knees, scrabbling about under the furniture with the bailiffs' men, until the clock struck five when Madame Humbert coolly pointed out that the bailiffs' writ had expired, their time was up, and they must leave, returning any stray pearls as they went.

But by the summer of 1901, odd rumors were starting to fly around Paris. A secret meeting of the Humberts' northern creditors broke up in disarray that autumn. Elie Cattaui of the Anglo-Egyptian Bank sued for repayment of a loan on which he had charged Madame Humbert 64.14 percent interest. In return she accused him of usury. Awkward questions were asked in the national newspapers. *Le Matin* chose this moment to mount a critical campaign, masterminded by F. I. Mouthon with help from the Girard receiver Duret, whose case reached the final Courts of Appeals in Paris early in 1902. People remembered Waldeck-Rousseau's phrase about the greatest swindle of the century. Creditors began to panic. Jacquin and the Humbert lawyers redoubled their denunciation of press calumny and lies. "You can tell how desperate they are by their very fury," Jacquin declared, confidently predicting total vindication for the Humberts. "Many of those who are now howling for their blood will no doubt then be the first to lick their feet."

The end came with a simple request from the appellate judge for the permanent domicile of the elusive Crawford brothers. Madame Humbert gave the first address that came into her head, 1302 Broadway. Investigations in New York reported no Crawfords at any such address. In response to the request of a creditor called Morel, the judge signed an order on Tuesday, May 6, for the strongbox to be opened three days later so that an inventory could be taken of its contents.

That night the Humberts drank a champagne toast, proposed by Thérèse herself with tears in her eyes, to the downfall of their adversaries. The name of Crawford was never mentioned in the Humbert household ("We only ever talked of "Madame's enemies," said Parayre). Thérèse's vivid sense of injury and persecution went back to her own and her family's misfortunes in Aussonne. Tears, help-lessness, a poignant projection of herself as victim were always her trump cards. "I am pursued by vil-lains [*Ze suis poursuivi par les mécants*]," had been her habitual refrain as a wide-eyed girl in Toulouse, trying out the lisp that nobody could resist. "Perhaps she's still saying it," one of her old dupes

The opening of the strongbox. *(Photo: © Collection Viollet, Paris)*

said drily when Madame Humbert's dreamworld finally collapsed, "with the same faulty pronunciation, and the same air of candor that used to work so well for her."

Thérèse left Paris on Wednesday, May 7, saying she needed a day's rest in the country. Her last act was to send around to her sister-in-law, Alice Daurignac, a watch engraved with her old defiant device—*Je veux, j'aurai*—and a card marked "Pardon!" From that moment she disappeared with her entire family into thin air. Cattaui formally charged her with fraud the next day.

❧❦❧

On Friday, the day set for the opening of the strongbox, crowds began assembling early outside 65, avenue de la Grande Armée. By midday there were ten thousand people in the street, controlled by a police squad under Lépine himself. The man in charge inside the house was the state prosecutor (also a family friend). The Parayres, bewildered by the absence of the Humberts, believed to the last that the safe was about to give up its millions. Locksmiths arrived with hammers when no key could be produced. Du Buit, who had been the last person to say good-bye to Madame Humbert, was among the first to fall back, white-faced and stony-eyed, from the empty strongbox, which contained nothing but an old newspaper, an Italian coin, and a trouser button.

The press grasped instantly that this was the sensational opening episode of a serial or soap

The removal of the strongbox.
(Photo: © Hulton Getty, London)

opera likely to run for months. "The *Figaro* can boast of having been present at the most staggering theatrical transformation scene that could have been thought up, even in a Paris so full of strange surprises, preposterous happenings, and absurd buffoonery," wrote the paper's star reporter on May 10, promising to keep his readers up-to-date with each fresh development in "the whole phantasmagoria of this incomparable novel."

Du Buit resigned a week later as leader of the bar, refusing to see or speak to reporters. "What humiliation the man must have endured," wrote Madame X, "having passed for so long as an *eagle* to find that many of his rivals now took him for a *goose.*" Jacquin also tendered his resignation in a humiliating letter (promptly published in the press) to the Minister of Justice, himself another Humbert regular, Monsieur Vallé. The leading lawyers involved on either side in the *Humbert* v. *Crawford* litigation were arrested on suspicion of fraud.

Interviews with shocked, disorientated, sometimes weeping creditors filled the front pages. The Rente Viagère was declared bankrupt. Thousands lost their life's savings. The press published lists, regularly updated, of those to whom the Humberts owed money, together with the staggering sums involved. Names ranged from the Empress Eugénie and the president's son, Paul Loubet, through bankers, lawyers, industrialists, and speculators to the great Parisian jewelers and diamond merchants, Roulina, Haas and Dumaret of the rue de la Paix. The body of a ruined investor called Aloyse Muller, who had committed suicide, was discovered on May 30. Dumaret, to whom Madame Humbert owed nearly two million francs, closed his shop and shot himself two weeks later.

"Scum!" "Cheats and hypocrites!" murmured the fashionable Parisians who piled into Georges Petit's smart art gallery to see the Humberts' picture collection sold that spring. The salesroom was dominated by Frédéric's state portrait of his father, Gustave Humbert (whose bust had already been discreetly removed from the university hall of honor in Toulouse). "All these luxurious leavings stink of grief and ruin, other people's ruin," wrote Jules Claretie, describing the poisonous atmosphere of rancor mixed with gloating among the crowd at Petit's. "You might think that these col-

"Roll up, roll up!! to see the Female Colossus THERESE, the world's greatest trickster: accompanied by the dwarf FREDERIC, painter, poet, musician, etc., etc., by her brother EMILE and by the handsome ROMAIN, striking a Roman pose. . . ." *(Private collection, all rights reserved; photo:*

ors had been ground up on the bodies of the victims. And you might ask nervously whether the vermilion in these paintings was mixed with blood."

The Humbert affair loomed over the next weeks and months, raising ominous echoes of the still recent Dreyfus affair. If the first had spelled disaster for the army, the second already looked likely to bring down the judiciary. "The entire public administration of Paris turned pale at the sight of the Humbert dossier," Arthur Huc wrote grimly. An anonymous judge observed that "Madame Humbert would prove a defendant quite as dangerous to others as to herself." People were beginning to wonder why Prefect Lépine (who had successfully organized Dreyfus's arrest) was failing so signally to find any trace of the Humberts. "What power restrains the hand of justice?" asked the *Télégramme* of Toulouse on May 24. "Whose orders have paralyzed the police force?"

The affair was rapidly developing along party lines. The current prime minister, René Waldeck-Rousseau, had been widely regarded by the left as the savior of the republic when he pardoned Captain Dreyfus in 1899. The year before that, Waldeck-Rousseau had been the first to denounce the Humberts in public as swindlers. But by 1902 he was a sick man, worn down by political struggle, with no stomach for taking on a scandal that would tear his party apart and probably destroy the reputation of one of its founding fathers into the bargain. On June 7, exactly a month after the opening of the strongbox, Rousseau was replaced by Emile Combes. A progressive Freemason (at least ten members of Combes's cabinet were Masons), whose chief priority was damage limitation, Combes let it be known that any officious pursuit or agitation would be discreetly discouraged.

❧❧

Madame Humbert had gone to ground with her husband; her daughter, Eve; and her siblings Emile, Romain, and Maria Daurignac. Sightings of various members of the family, popping up that summer here and there all over Europe, led to nothing. After six months there had been no

The Spanish police eventually discover the Humberts'
hideout. *(Photo: © Mary Evans Picture Library, London)*

progress whatsoever in tracking down the fugitives. On December 6 the matter was raised in the
Chamber of Deputies. Questions were asked as to
why the head of the police force, the attorney
general, and the justice minister—all Humbert
associates—were still holding their jobs. "This was

the signal for the kind of violent uproar we saw not long ago when questions were asked about the Dreyfus affair," reported *Le Matin* next day. Fights broke out among the deputies, developing into such a riot that the session had to be suspended three times and finally abandoned altogether. Right-wingers, who interpreted the Humbert affair as a left-wing conspiracy, did their best to implicate Madame Humbert in the Dreyfus scandal, or better still hold her personally responsible for it, on the grounds that her creditors included Dreyfus's father-in-law, the diamond merchant Alfred Hadamard. The charges were taken up with enthusiasm by the right-wing press ("The *Sun* made a mistake in not offering a live rabbit and six dozen macaroons to the joker who can make any sense of this ludicrous rigmarole," Huc wrote crisply).

Within two weeks of the parliamentary brawl, the Humberts were discovered in hiding in Madrid. Their arrests on December 20 were reported under banner headlines in the newspapers. Vast crowds assembled at the station on December 29 to see the family brought back to

Thérèse Humbert.   Eva Humbert   Maria Daurignac

Police mug shots of the suspects under arrest.
(Photo: © Jean-Loup Charmet, Paris).

Humbert toys on sale in Paris.
(Photo: © Mary Evans Picture Library, London)

ARISTOCRATS OF CRIME: The Humberts return to Paris.
(Photo: © Mary Evans Picture Library, London)

Paris under police escort. "Give back the money, you old witch!" cried a workman watching Thérèse disembark, flanked by two detectives. The prisoners were locked up in separate cells in the Conciergerie (Thérèse's was opposite the cell that, just over a century earlier, had held Marie Antoinette).

Paris went wild with excitement that Christmas. People whistled ribald pop songs with titles like *The Humberts' Christmas*. Clockwork toys hawked on the streets included tiny Madame Humberts selling Spanish oranges, or escaping through the back windows of Spanish hideouts, pursued by the police with trails of banknotes fluttering behind. There was a Humbert board game, and a rubber balloon in the shape of a long thin Romain Daurignac who burst when you blew him up, deflating with a low moaning wail. Caricatures depicted the Humberts as a family theatrical troupe starring in melodramas called *Humbugs' Heritage* or *The Secrets of the Strongbox*. Sometimes they were a circus team or a conjuring act, with Thérèse strutting in the center as a whip-cracking ringmaster or wand-waving magician.

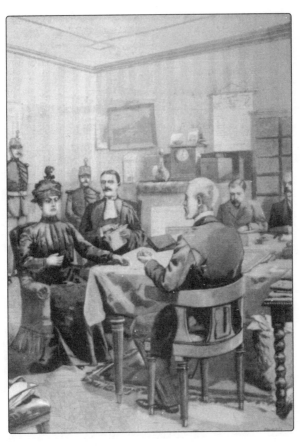

Interrogation of Madame Humbert.
(Photo: © Mary Evans Picture Library, London)

Madame Humbert takes command of the legal team.
(Photo: © Topham Picturepoint)

Something of this circus atmosphere carried over into the judicial interrogation in the new year of 1903. Top billing was reserved for a series of electric confrontations between the Humbert duo and the couple they had callously left to hold the bag for them, Monsieur and Madame Parayre. In the six months between the Humberts' disappearance and their arrest, "Parayre" had become a household word throughout France for infamy and shame. Lacking anyone else to blame, the press and public cast Armand Parayre as their scapegoat when the scandal first broke in May. His wife, who collapsed with misery and shock, was demonized in the popular prints as "the Cerberus of 65, avenue de la Grande Armée" or "Madame Humbert's evil genius." Policemen searched their apartment for incriminating evidence before sealing it, along with the rest of the Humberts' house. The hat shop belonging to their daughter, Amélie Matisse, was also raided. So was her husband's studio. The Parayres eventually fled Paris to take refuge in the tiny house of their younger daughter, Berthe, where detectives kept them under surveillance from a blind across the street.

Catherine Parayre confronting her
old friend and betrayer in court.
(Photo: Alice Mackenzie)

At Christmas 1902 Armand Parayre was arrested and imprisoned in a cell in the Conciergerie alongside the fugitives from Madrid. In January he was brought before the magistrate to face the Humberts for the first time since he had toasted the downfall of their enemies with them the previous May. Frédéric fainted under cross-examination, and had to be carried out of court. Thérèse flushed dark red when her former employee refused to take the hand she held out to him. Parayre's dignity and resolution impressed the magistrate, and calmed the spectators who had anticipated something more like a confrontation between snarling lions. On January 31, after six weeks in jail and a grueling public interrogation, he was set free and his name disappeared at last from the front pages of the newspapers.

❧

The proceedings continued to absorb the public all through the spring, with the trial itself promised for the summer. Observers compared the twists and turns of the dramatically unfolding plot to a

Captain Dreyfus's defense counsel, the great Maître Labori, center stage, with his clients Monsieur and Madame Humbert and Emile Daurignac in the dock behind him. *(Photo: © Jean-Loup Charmet, Paris)*

play, a novel in installments, or a serial thriller. All agreed that for pure inventiveness, the facts outstripped the wildest romantic fiction. Even her harshest critics conceded that Thérèse was beyond belief. F. I. Mouthon, whose investigative campaign had helped to precipitate her downfall, now found something Homeric about the sheer scale of operations that "raised burglary . . . to the height of a work of genius."

Thérèse herself rose to the occasion. At times she seemed positively to revel in it. In August 1903 she was finally brought to trial with her husband and two brothers (Maria Daurignac and Eve Humbert had been set free) before the Assize Court of the Seine. Fashionable Paris filled the courtroom. The solicitor general, Maître Blondel, opened for the prosecution, with Dreyfus's celebrated counsel, Maître Labori, retained by the defense. Thérèse faced a packed house with the masklike pallor and fiercely controlled energy of a great actress. "Beneath sharply incised brows, her great black eyes, dilated with battle fever, burned with a strange fire," wrote *Le Matin*'s Stéphane Lauzanne: "we were watching one of the most fantastic and one of the most gripping judicial spectacles it would be possible to see."

All eyes were riveted by Thérèse giving the last, in some ways the most dramatic, and certainly the most desolating performance of her life. Her voice regained its old mesmeric quality: husky, febrile, at times imperious but always with an

The international press reported a packed house in court for the last act of the Humbert Show. *(Photo: © Hulton Getty, London)*

undertone of pleading. People whom she had duped and exploited found they still could not entirely resist her spell. Maître Dumort of Rouen—who had lost his name, his reputation, and his law practice as well as every penny he possessed—confessed that he had been hypnotized. So did the distiller from Lille, Jean Schotmann, whose brother, Paul, had been shot when he refused the Humberts a second loan. Schotmann described how he had traveled up to Paris to see Madame Humbert after the murder, determined not to part with another *sou*, and found himself persuaded against his will not only to shell out a further two million francs, but to impersonate an imaginary Humbert uncle into the bargain. "I admit I was dumbfounded, but my surprise was so great that I did not protest. Since then I have come to realize that I was playing a part in a play, but I still can't explain how it happened."

Witness after witness testified to Thérèse's magic powers. People talked of her as a sorcerer or an enchantress ("With what composure she understood when to be vigilant, or haughty, or bewitching: how to tame and subjugate her subjects"). At one point a witness tried to assault Maître Labori. Cattaui's testimony degenerated into Punch-and-Judy name-calling, with cries of "Liar! Vampire! Wretch!" countered by: "Master blackmailer!" and "Crook!" During the prosecution's closing speech, Romain staged a nosebleed so copious that the courtroom had to be washed down. But few had eyes for anything save the spectacle of Thérèse as a hunted creature, trapped by the prosecutor's relentless exposure. "She experienced—and so did the public craning forward at the ringside to watch this unequal duel—the bitter and painful sensation that she was lost, that she was enclosed within a circle of fire drawing ever more tightly round her," wrote Lauzanne. "Until at last, definitively brought down, crushed on a scale beyond the dreams of her worst enemies, breathless and exhausted, like an animal captured and cowering on the ground, she almost fell into the arms of the warders who carried her out—as you might toss away a bundle of rags."

All observers agreed that Thérèse ended up as limp and woebegone as a deflated rubber toy. She and her husband were each sentenced to five years' solitary confinement with hard labor. Emile and Romain got two and three years respectively. None of the Humberts' lawyers ever practiced again, but no further charges were brought, and no attempt was made to look more closely at the web of corruption that had briefly been uncovered. The limited nature of the proceedings and the relative lightness of the sentences suggest that some sort of deal had been struck behind the scenes. If so, the Humberts kept their side of it. Thérèse served her sentence in the women's prison at Rennes. Frédéric served his at Melun, where he had once triumphed

Thérèse Humbert awaiting sentence in her cell in the Conciergerie. *(Photo: Alice Mackenzie)*

as a deputy. She was fifty-two years old and he was fifty-one when they were released. Nothing more was ever heard of either of them.

❧

The Humbert affair was barely mentioned again in history books, or personal memoirs. Those who suffered worst—top bankers, senior politicians, jurists like Du Buit, Jacquin, and Dumort who had believed in the Humberts to the end— had most to gain from keeping their humiliation quiet. Although Armand Parayre kept his nerve, his wife, Catherine, never recovered from the destruction of her faith in Thérèse, which was also her faith in herself. She lived just long enough to see her son-in-law, Henri Matisse, publicly reviled as a charlatan and confidence trickster. From 1905, on the strength of his showing at the Autumn Salon in Paris, Matisse was nicknamed "the Wild Beast" [or *le Fauve*] and his work was regularly dismissed by critics as an attempt to pull a fast one on the public. His wife, whose belief in him never wavered, repeated her mother's advice to pay no

La Grande Thérèse, stripped at last of all her trappings.
(Photo: Alice Mackenzie)

attention to the newspapers, but Catherine Parayre died in 1908, long before the world conceded that her son-in-law was a genuine magician after all.

A single observer in her lifetime attempted an aesthetic defense of Thérèse Humbert, arguing that hers was an imagination whose inventions sprang from the basic creative instinct to reshape experience. "If she had never left the South, none of this would have happened," wrote *Le Matin*'s columnist, H. Harduin:

> Madame Humbert was only trying to give herself a little of that illusion which is essential to cover up the miseries of existence, if you are poor. She thought she was at home, she didn't realize there would be people in the North stupid enough or credulous enough not to make allowances, not to take into account that element of fantasy, of imagination, without which reality seems too bare and harsh. . . . Madame Humbert forgot that what isn't necessarily true in the South is taken literally in the North, where you can't tell lies without being immediately believed.

Otherwise virtually no one had a good word to say for la Grande Thérèse, who had started out as a little girl telling fairy stories, and ended up being denounced by a procession of industrialists and bankers taking the witness stand in Paris, and

"Ah! poor Thérèse! You've gobbled up a hundred
million, and now you'll have to gobble beans."

(Private collection, all rights reserved;
photo: © MT-Giraudon, Paris)

on the front pages of the national and international press. Some were contemptuous, others savagely angry. But many were not so much vindictive as rueful, incredulous, still half bewitched when they gave their evidence that August, rubbing their eyes and blinking, like people waking from a dream to find that their fairy gold had turned into dry leaves.

Epilogue

I **first came across** la Grande Thérèse by chance seven years ago, in the course of research in and around Toulouse for a biography of Henri Matisse. Her story astounded me, and not simply because of the drastic impact her exposure—or rather the devastation it brought to his wife's family—had on Matisse's life. When I came to write the first volume of my biography, I had to fight so hard to relegate Thérèse to a minor role that, once it was finished, I felt I owed her a book of her own.

Having served her term of five years' hard labor, Thérèse vanished as completely as if she had never been. No one knows what happened after her release in 1908: where she lived, or how, or under what name, not even when and why she died. There were no interviews in her lifetime, and no obituaries to mark her end. It was admittedly not in the interest of the state to expose the Humberts to attention at a time when France had still not fully recovered from the Dreyfus scandal. Contemporaries freely admitted that, if the Dreyfus affair had knocked the stuffing out of the right wing and the army, the Humbert affair seemed likely to do the same for the left and its civil administration. The practical threat to the judiciary was compounded by the moral contamination that put the honor of the republic itself at stake. Prime Minister Waldeck-Rousseau was not alone in harboring grave misgivings about a criminal investigation almost certain to end up implicating one of his regime's founding fathers.

It was left to Waldeck-Rousseau's successor to preside over an exercise in damage limitation that has proved wholly successful from that day to this. Senator Humbert's involvement in the affair that bears his name has never before been closely examined (suggestive details previously ignored include, for instance, the fact that he was Thérèse's uncle by marriage as well as her father-in-law). His reputation remains intact in histories of the period, including the official *Dictionnaire de la biographie française* (on reaching *H* with its fifth and last volume in 1994). Thérèse herself is remembered dimly, if at all, as the heroine of a grotesquely comic episode briefly outlined in popular histories of great French fraudsters.

In 1993, when I crossed her tracks by accident while talking to local people in her native region, she seemed hardly definite enough to be a memory: more of a vague, capricious, insubstantial figment waiting in some transit lounge of limbo to be finally absorbed into folk myth. That first encounter sent me straight to the departmental reference library in Toulouse to find out more about her from newspaper reports and interviews published at the turn of the century. A friend who was with me ordered bound volumes of *Le Télégramme,* and I settled down with the city's famous radical organ, *La Dépêche.* We turned the pages with mounting incredulity.

❧❧❧

La Grande Thérèse may read like a fairy tale but I have invented nothing. The facts laid out here, together with every word of dialogue, come from contemporary sources. Toulouse's local press contains marvellously rich and detailed first-hand accounts of Thérèse's origins and character by people who had known her all her life. No one has ever drawn on them before. Previous versions of her story have been based almost exclusively on the Paris papers, which accurately reflect the widespread revulsion and contempt inspired by her downfall at the time. I have tried to trace Thérèse back to her beginnings, and to show her in her prime in the munificent Paris of the Belle Epoque when she and her family were far from the bedraggled fugitives who turned up in the dock in 1903 to be pelted with mud by all and sundry.

❧❧❧

There is some question as to whether Thérèse was her parents' firstborn child: one or two witnesses claimed her brother Emile as the elder of the two, other accounts suggest there may have been an even older sister (possibly fathered by Madame Daurignac's phantom Portuguese lover), who died young. Thérèse herself made much play with this alter ego, also called Thérèse, but the court ruled out her existence at the Humbert trial in 1903.

I would like to thank Marie-José Gransard for much help and guidance in the initial stages of research in 1993. My main sources have been the following newspapers during the period after the scandal broke (May–July 1902), the arrest and interrogation (December 1902-July 1903), and the trial itself (August 1903): *La Dépêche* and *Le Télégramme,* Toulouse; *Le Matin, Le Figaro,* and *La Gazette des Tribuneaux,* Paris; *Le Journal de Rouen* and *L'Indépendant de Cambrésis.*

Further accounts of the Humbert affair can be found in: *Thérèse Intime. Souvenirs de Mme. X* (anon., Paris, 1903); *La Vie à Paris* by Jules Claretie (Paris, 1904); *Notes sur la justice républicaine,* by Henri Dutrait-Crozon (Paris, 1924); *La Belle Affaire* by H. Vonoven, Paris, 1925; *Famous*

Crimes of Recent Times, by Edgar Wallace, William Le Queux, et al. (London, n.d.); *Le Roman vrai de la 3e République*, vol. 1, *Prelude à la Belle Epoque*, ed. G. Guilleminault (Paris, 1956); and *Histoires d'Escrocs*, by Adam Pianko (Paris, 1997). The relevant chapter in *The Hypocrisy of Justice in the Belle Epoque,* by Benjamin F. Martin (Louisiana, 1984) is the only serious attempt I know of to investigate the political implications of the affair; and another previously unknown side effect is explored in my own *The Unknown Matisse: A Life of Henri Matisse, The Early Years, 1869–1908* (New York, 1998).